SCHOLASTIC
**News**
Nonfiction Readers

# Madam C. J. Walker

## by
## Catherine Nichols

Children's Press®
A Division of Scholastic Inc.
New York  Toronto  London  Auckland  Sydney
Mexico City  New Delhi  Hong Kong
Danbury, Connecticut

These content vocabulary word builders
are for grades 1-2.

Consultant: Dr. Tiffany M. Gill
Professor of History
University of Texas at Austin

Curriculum Specialist: Linda Bullock

Photo Credits:

Photographs © 2005: A'Lelia Bundles/Walker Family Collection/madamcjwalker.com: 4 bottom left 13, 20 bottom (Indiana Historical Society), 5 bottom left, 15, 21 top (Sylvia Jones), 19, 21 bottom right (Walt Thomas), back cover, 3, 4 bottom right, 5 top left, 5 top right, 5 bottom right, 6, 9, 10, 11, 17, 20 top, 21 bottom left; AP/Wide World Photos: 23 top right; Corbis Images/Underwood & Underwood: 23 bottom right; Getty Images/John Kobal Foundation/Hulton Archive: 23 bottom left; Indiana Historical Society Library: front cover; Library of Congress: 1, 4 top, 7, 16; The Western Reserve Historical Society, Cleveland, OH: 23 top left.

Book Design: Simonsays Design!

Library of Congress Cataloging-in-Publication Data

Nichols, Catherine.
    Madam C.J. Walker / by Catherine Nichols.
       p. cm. — (Scholastic news nonfiction readers)
    Includes bibliographical references and index.
    ISBN 0-516-24941-X (lib. bdg.)          0-516-24784-0 (pbk.)
    1. Walker, C. J., Madam, 1867-1919—Juvenile literature. 2. African
       American women executives—Biography—Juvenile literature. 3.
       Women millionaires—United States—Biography—Juvenile literature.
       4. Cosmetics industry—United States—History-Juvenile literature. 5.
       Walker, C. J., Madam, 1867-1919. [1. Businesspeople.] I. Title. II.
       Series.
    HD9970.5.C672W357 2005
    338.7'66855'092—dc22

                                                        2005002084

# CONTENTS

# WORD HUNT

Look for these words as you read. They will be in **bold**.

**ad**
(ad)

**factory**
(**fak**-tuh-ree)

**hair grower**
(hair **groh**-ur)

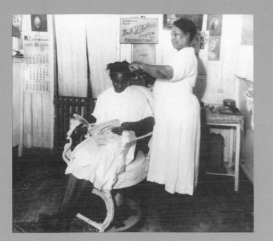

**beauty salon**
(**byoo**-tee suh-**lawn**)

**cabin**
(**kab**-in)

**sales agents**
(sales **ay**-juhnts)

**shampoo**
(sham-**poo**)

5

# Meet Madam Walker

Madam C. J. Walker was born in a **cabin** on December 23, 1867.

She lived in Delta, Louisiana.

**Walker's cabin**

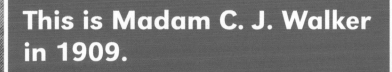

This is Madam C. J. Walker in 1909.

Madam Walker was always interested in hair.

Madam Walker did not like to buy hair-care products in the stores.

Those products did not work on her hair.

Madam Walker made her own hair-care products.

She mixed together herbs and oils.

She made **shampoo**, **hair grower**, and other hair-care products.

**hair grower**

shampoo

Walker sold her products to other African American women.

She put her products on their hair.

The women liked the way their hair looked.

Walker was in business! She opened a **factory** to make her products.

**Madam Walker's factory was
in Indianapolis, Indiana.**

13

Madam Walker hired other women to sell her products, too.

They were called **sales agents**.

The sales agents went door-to-door to sell Walker's products.

**These sales agents worked with Madam Walker.**

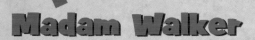

Madam Walker

Madam Walker put **ads** in newspapers to sell her products, too.

She showed pictures of herself in the ads.

She opened many **beauty salons** and beauty schools.

ad

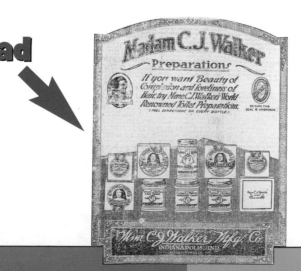

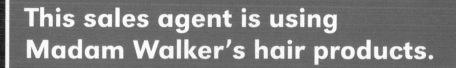

This sales agent is using
Madam Walker's hair products.

Walker made a lot of money selling her products.

She used some of it to help other people.

Madam Walker did many great things in her life.

She died on May 25, 1919.

Today, Madam Walker's picture is on a stamp.

# Madam C. J. Walker

**1** Madam C. J. Walker is born in Louisiana on December 23, 1867.

**2** In the early 1900's, Walker invents a hair grower.

**3** In 1910, Walker builds a factory where she makes her products.

**5** Here is Walker with some of her sales agents in 1918.

On May 25, 1919, Walker dies. Here is a stamp with her picture on it!

**6**

**4** Madam C. J. Walker begins opening beauty salons and beauty schools.

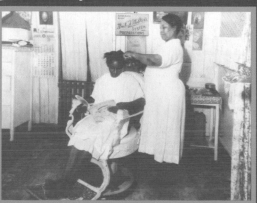

BLACK HERITAGE

32 USA

Madam C. J. Walker

# YOUR NEW WORDS

**ad** (ad)  something that tries to get you to buy a product

**beauty salon** (**byoo**-tee suh-**lawn**)  a place where people go to have their hair done

**cabin** (**kab**-in)  a small house

**factory** (**fak**-tuh-ree)  a place where things are made

**hair grower** (hair **groh**-ur) a product that helps hair grow

**sales agents** (sales **ay**-juhnts)  people who sell products

**shampoo** (sham-**poo**) a product used to clean hair

# Other American Inventors

**Garrett Morgan invented the gas mask.**

**George Washington Carver invented peanut products.**

**Hedy Lamarr invented a secret code.**

**Lillian Gilbreth invented an electric food mixer.**

# INDEX

## FIND OUT MORE
**Book:**
*Vision of Beauty: The Story of Sarah Breedlove Walker*
by Kathryn Lasky (Candlewick Press, 2003)

**Website:**
The Black Inventor Online Museum
www.blackinventor.com

## MEET THE AUTHOR
**Catherine Nichols** is the author of many books for young readers. She especially likes to write biographies. Catherine also wrote the Sally Ride biography in the *Scholastic News Nonfiction Readers* series.